Donna The Book (www.donnathebook.com) is where I opened my heart and share our story of a life-time of touching and magical memories, focusing not only on the journey from terminal diagnosis to death, before we met, and my life after death.

This book is dedicated to you, Donna,
to the memories we created, and the
memories I didn't know existed. Your
death does not keep me from living.

I am keeping you from dying because...
closure is indifference. It is denial said pretty.
Closure is unfair to you and to us because
my memories and the grief lead me to
wisdom, understanding, and love.

Memories are not fiction,
they are everlasting gifts we
continue to give each other.

DONNA

MARK DIMOR

PREFACE

As a child, sometimes I sat on a
workbench in the metal plating plant
where my father worked in sales.

One day I found a vial of mercury,
opened it, and poured it on the bench.

I played with the mercury, my fingers gently pushing around these shimmering reflective drops like silver Jello.

The drops touched then suddenly embraced to create a bigger drop. Each drop grew as it touched another until there was one large mass of silver bouncing on the bench ever so slightly.

I picked up a screwdriver, struck the mercury, and watched it splinter and scatter into hundreds of little drops.

Then I repeated the entire exercise, building up one large reflection, over and over.

Those shattered drops are my shimmering strewn memories of my wife, Donna.

At 6 p.m. on August 7, 2011, two hours after Donna died, I called a friend to tell him.

"Don't deny or run from your pain and grief," he said. "Examine it and live with it. That's the only way to find a way through."

At that moment I became an active participant in my grieving, which began two and half years earlier when Donna was diagnosed with Stage IV cancer.

I am still actively grieving, and memories are threatening to pull me under. I need new thoughts and consciousness. Reflecting on our experience out loud to the world might provide that.

But there are limits to sharing my memories of her. They won't tell her entire story; they're just a few coins jangling in the cup of a beggar. Like photos, they have no depth. Only the remembering creates depth and context.

All that remains are the grief-scented memories, and the desire to rearrange them into one single reflection. Maybe it will have meaning. Maybe its light will guide me. That's my hope.

IN THE BEGINNING

Closure is indifference.

It is denial said pretty.

I won't do it. It's unfair to Donna.

Closure removes the chance to
find meaning in her life and death.

When she was diagnosed I began to grieve. Seven-plus years later, this state of grief is the emotional inertia I live with. It resists change but I need to find the potential these memories hold.

                    I have to be cautious, though.
                    I can't obscure the reality.

We put up a Christmas tree every year.
The simple, plain Douglass Fir was
complete in and of itself.

    The branches and needles, perfectly green and symmetrical, were majestic and sublime. Then the decorations transformed it into an object of celebration and life. The lights, ornaments, and tinsel, in the right balance and placement, made that simple tree a grand memory. It was a genesis, the single, indelible moment when Christmas began and all our small joys reflected and shone more brightly.

Add too much tinsel, it would
become garish, despoiling the tree.

I don't want to do that to Donna.

Donna was sitting in the bullpen at a drafting table, doing mechanicals. She was wearing arched, blocky Candie's heels with purple socks and a long skirt, but it was that hair that made the moment. Without the hair, great fashion sense. With the hair, style.

No bells rang. I didn't suddenly feel a future
coming on. Yet my days began to bend around
the couple of square feet of her drafting table.

I walked past her frequently, listening to
the slap of the T-square on the table, the
zip of the X-Acto knife across a type
proof, the brushing of two-coat on the
type. I peeked at her precise placement of
mortised six-point brief disclosure type,
lined up to the pica. All done without
glasses. Her motions were fluid as a
maestro's, nothing haphazard, directing
her inner orchestra to create perfection.

The intensity on her face: be still,
my heart. Be as still as her fingers
for the last micro-alignment.

Back then it was fine to flirt, to be a d-bag.
I would stand over Donna, watching her work.
Once I massaged her shoulders.

"I am holding an X-Acto knife," she said.
"You want me to cut you?"

I wasn't afraid to do it again. That was my saving grace with Donna. I was never afraid of her. For some reason she valued my confidence.

I was not a great boyfriend prior to meeting her and, I'm sure she would say, not for a long time after. My mother had this speech she'd give girls I brought home during high school and college.

"You know, my son is a wonderful, kind boy. He will charm you. He is good and will be good to you but I know him, how I raised him, and my effect on him. He will break your heart, not from cruelty or hurt feelings but from boredom. You will watch him turn inattentive to you and you'll blame yourself for his selfishness and then it will hurt worse."

Donna never got the speech. My mother
saw immediately how she challenged me
and knew I would never be bored.

The two of them took perverse joy in putting me
in my place. At family gatherings they made sure I
knew my job: keep their coffee or drinks or plates
filled. They corrected my malaprops as fast as I
made them. The best was when I would pepper
my language with big words, or any words for that
matter, and they would say, "Spell that for us."

I adored Donna's strength and brains as I had adored my mother's. Growing up in a largely matriarchal family where both parents had to work to keep a roof over our heads, my brother, sister, and I were taught the basics of cooking, cleaning, laundry, and housework. One day I complained to Mom about why I had to do this stuff. With the impeccable logic of a woman raising sons she said, "I don't want you to get married for the wrong reasons. You marry for love."

Donna was not domestic. I was. Donna was beautiful, smart, feared no one, and believed in herself. I loved that. I could do the rest. Maybe she would help me to learn from her.

We all know that dating is a slow dance of expectations and considerations. One two, one two, turn and step. I was genuinely struck by Donna's art direction, the entire creative process and theory. How do you create something from nothing yet send a message that actually drives behavior?

It was the late '70s but it wasn't about clubs or discos for us. We dated through art, type, and advertising. So many of our conversations were about type, typefaces, type placement, what type does and what it can't do. The message was always in the type. For Donna it was the most important consideration. Size, spacing, kerning, length of headlines, size of headlines, fonts used for headlines, fonts used for body copy, line breaks, widows and white space—a layout was her calculus. It was all about drawing the eye to the page, keeping it there, and imprinting it with an image, an idea.

She saw the world as she saw type on a page: what is not there says as much as what is. The white spaces are pauses and silence. She did not want to fill the page or her world with clutter. This meant that if you were included in her world, you knew you were emphatically important. You were part of her statement.

"This is a test," she said. "Type-spec a manuscript for a layout."

I did as well as I could.

"Good," she said, and kept me in her world.

We dated, lived together, broke up twice. Friends of mine pointed out that I was GU (geographically undesirable) by living in Washington Heights, a damn long ride on the A Train. Yet the first time we lived together, Donna gave up an apartment on East 86th Street and rode the A train every morning. It was years before I realized the level of sacrifice she'd made. She was not a morning person and believed cabs were a little square of heaven on earth.

The second time we lived together, still in Washington Heights, we bought our first apartment. It was on the top floor and overlooked the Hudson River, New Jersey, and the George Washington Bridge. The apartment was wonderfully light and airy and faced south. Afternoons were brilliant and warm and demanded naps, especially after coming in from a cold winter. It was ours and it was home.

As perfect as the space was, I was not. My ego and selfishness prevailed. Neither of us would back down from a fight. No prisoners, no peace. She moved out to a walkup in Soho and I found a note from her left on a shelf in our small office.

"No one will love
you like I do."

I started sitting at a bar in Soho near where she lived, looking out the window, hoping to see her walk by.

It never happened.

I was one of the walking wounded. In Los Angeles on business, my boss spent one entire afternoon and evening between appointments driving me around, showing me the sights and talking with me. After twilight he took me to Griffith Observatory overlooking L.A., the stars above and the lights below all twinkling.

> I knew I needed to find
> a way back to Donna.

I changed and I talked to Donna and I changed some
more. I'd always been attentive and interested in
her, never bored. Now I began to learn that I could
be alone and be me and not self-loathe. I accepted
that I was not surrendering me to be with her—I
was becoming me. Ripping away some of my ego, I
found underneath, the person she loved.

And she wasn't sacrificing herself to me,
even while feeding the best parts of myself.

If you can't see her drive and focus in these photographs, you're missing out. They were the best parts of her.

Her drive was different from competition, though. She didn't compete. She didn't need to. I saw that in every choice she made. With her clothes, she wasn't dressing for other women. It was simply, this is me, this is my expression and art of me.

"Anyone can buy fashion," she'd say. "Not everyone can buy style."

That was the road map for our life together. She told me what colors I could purchase for the apartment: grey or black, but confirm everything prior. If the spectrum was involved, she'd hand me Pantone chips before I shopped. Donna's direction of our space and visual life did not provoke my wanting control or damage my maleness. It just felt right.

At least the pictures catch her smile, her admission of the camera and me into a world seen only by the people she loved.

After her death her friends said the same thing over and over, "I was thrilled to be allowed into Donna's life. She did so much to help me with my career. Very few were there and it was special for me. She gave from the heart."

> For thirty years I stayed
> amazed that she let me in.

I rehearse my failures daily. Could I
have done more or been more of what
I see now in myself? Over 28 years of
marriage, of course I failed, as humans
do. It's less about leaving socks on
the floor or squeezing the toothpaste
from the wrong end. Maybe I could
have listened more, been more present,
been less frustrated with my life and
kept it from spilling over on our life.
If I'd been less reactive, less worried
about the future…

                                        I don't know.

I was her polar opposite and that must have weighed on her. She supremely believed in her instincts and everything she did. Frequently she would tell me to trust mine. I never really did.

Reflection isn't all it's cracked up to be.
Memories are intended to be comforting;
this feels like an aching to do better. I
can't go back to try.

Even if I could, she was complete.
She didn't need anything from me.
And yet she let me in.

At her funeral I said, "I read
somewhere that it's not how you
feel about someone; it's how they
make you feel about yourself."

How did I earn that smile, that love, from someone so intense? I'm not sure I deserved it. I'm not sure I deserve to have these memories and survive. Maybe every memory should have been scraped from my neurons when I learned she was dying. I struggle daily to be the me that Donna loved.

30 YEARS OF WE

```
      T ID 081 0809)(4-2032995 076)PD  03/17/82 080
ICS IPMMIZZ CSP
  2125933 330TDMT NEW YORK NY 7 03-17 0836A EST
PMS DONNA HERSH, PERSONAL DLY ONLY, DLR 11AM T
CARE KALLIR PHILIPS ROSS
505 THIRD AVE
NEW YORK NY 10158
 I LOVE YOU WILL YOU MARRY ME
   MARK                                05/03/2012
NNNN
```

On March 17, 1982, I sent a Western
Union Telegram to Donna at her office.

Yes, a telegram. I was not drunk.

I love you. Will you marry me.

May 5th, I received a telegram.

```
TIB190(1146)(1-013990A132)PD 05/12/82 1144
ICS IPMDCNA
01022 FR DC NEWYORK NY 2 05-12 1241P EDT
ICS IPM3ITI
MARK DIMOR, DELIVER C/O LAVEY, WOLF, SWIFT INC
488 MADISON AVE 20TH FLOOR
NEW YORK NY 10022
O.K.
LOVE,
 D.
NNNN
```

Ok. Love, D.

To the point, nothing in excess,
and completed when she wanted
to complete it, always on her terms.

> I had never asked anyone to marry
> me. I never wanted to. And the one
> I wanted to marry said yes.

This was our third time living together. We were
now on MacDougal Street, south of Houston
Street in old Soho, in a small, working-class block
of walkups. We lived on a fifth floor with old,
creaking, extra-wide stairs so families could move
in with pianos, yet the apartment was tiny. In one
room I could touch the north and south walls at
the same time. The bathroom was in the kitchen
and only recently given a wall with a door.

Did she need two months to consider
her answer? We were living together! The
telegram was never discussed, just a simple
"that's cute." It didn't hang over my head
or hers like a major life decision. It just felt
like, okay, we'll get to it.

Life went on. We'd drop off our laundry at the Chinese laundry on Thompson Street, where they not only washed and folded our sheets but ironed them. Then we'd stop by Joe's Dairy, one of the oldest cheese stores in NYC. Fresh mozzarella, both regular and smoked, was made daily.

"Don't say mozzarella," Donna said. "Say mutz."

All right, Jersey girl.

That block of Thompson was where the street fair in The Godfather was shot, and to this day the church on the block, Saint Anthony's, still holds that fair.

Donna and I were still trying to find our footing with ourselves and each other and as a couple. I corrected a lot of my overbearing personality since it was obvious there was no way to control or bully Donna, and I didn't want that anyway. I still had my worries, though. Growing up with Depression-era parents, I gnawed over money, savings, and spending. Donna grew up watching her mother worry over the same things but she spun the other way. Her growing success and ever-increasing income were reasons to be optimistic. She believed she could work more to earn more and if she couldn't, she knew how to live poor and happy. Me? The future was a glass half-empty and the other half was poison.

One evening after work, Donna came home with shopping bags of clothes and shoes. I went into a nagging rant about saving, the future, our lives together. At that time I was making significantly less than she but I kept going on and on and on. So she threw a glass ashtray at me. It hit a picture frame behind me, shattered the glass, and cut a gash in the back of my head.

Head wounds bleed. I bled. In the emergency room at St. Vincent's I got four stitches. Donna lost it, she was so upset, and begged my forgiveness. I fell even more in love, not because of the asking for forgiveness, but because she took no shit.

Christmas 1982, I bought Donna a pair of Elsa Peretti ¼-carat diamond studs. Up to this point, she was not the big-diamond type of woman. We never stopped in front of Tiffany's so she could point out the cut or size she liked. Diamonds were something other people got worked up about. These earrings were just set in plain 22-carat gold and well designed, and Donna lit up. She opened the box and immediately put them on, saying, "These are wonderful but let's not tell anyone we're engaged."

I wasn't quite sure what to make of that, but she knew. This was us. No need or desire for a dramatic public statement. We'd seen too many couples use extreme displays of affection to reinforce a structural weakness in their love.

    So she wore the earrings and we were engaged. Secretly engaged, so it could be revoked at any point.

Many, if not most, of our casual friends thought we'd never survive when they finally heard we were engaged. Yet we were married for 28 years. I knew what we had; she knew what we had. It was not some grand vision. It was more an acceptance and belief that this seemed like a good experiment. No need to painstakingly weigh and measure it. It just felt right.

So at some point early in 1983, we made plans for our wedding. We found a location, 65 Irving Place at 18th Street. In deference to Donna's mother, we tracked down a rabbi. We selected a menu. The only thing I remember from it was the flourless chocolate cake adorned with a bedazzled piece of art made by a friend. The bride and groom standing under a chuppah were Calaveras. It was us.

With a couple of weeks to go, I organized the blood tests and our birth certificates to take to the Marriage Bureau. Staring at her birth certificate, I realized her date of birth was February 14th. We had always celebrated her birthday on Valentine's Day.

"I always thought that was an affect," I told her. "You were actually born that day?"

She rolled her eyes and married me anyway. Well, almost.

I stood in line with my number at the
Marriage Bureau which, like all NYC public
offices, was plain, utilitarian, and drab. A clerk
called me to his window, started checking
through my documents, and tapped at his
computer. Then he looked up at me.

"Do you know your bride is married?
She never got divorced."

Huh? I knew she was married once. I never
asked if she ever got divorced. She didn't think
about it, I guess. In her world, the marriage was
over in her mind so it was over for everybody.

Donna spent the next week scurrying about to find her first husband, Jimmy, line up a lawyer, and get divorce papers drawn up. When I asked her about the marriage she delivered her usual mantra about her past: "There's a reason they call it history. It happened then."

But she gave me the thumbnail-sketch version. Her mother found Donna's birth control when she was seventeen and told her she had to get married, so Donna did and she lived with Jimmy in her mother's basement in New Jersey. One day Donna asked Jimmy if she could borrow his car. He said yes and she drove to San Francisco to start over in advertising.

Eventually, Jimmy found her in San Francisco and came out to see her and get the car. As he was driving out of the city the cops stopped the car and booked him on scofflaw violations. Apparently, Donna didn't consider parking tickets important. And that was her first marriage. I hoped that wasn't foreshadowing for her second.

Jimmy came over to our apartment and I wasn't sure what to expect, but he brought their dog—Pippin, named after a hobbit—and he was chill. It was actually fun to meet him. Maybe that did bode well for her second round.

We were married on May 15, 1983. All during the wedding prep I would tease her about the word "wife." I'd stutter it, "w-w-w-w-wife." It was my way of dropping the baggage that came with the word. In fact, during our 28 years, I rarely said "wife." It was always Donna. In my mind, a wife is a possession. Donna was a peer, a friend, a partner in my life, our life. She was simply Donna—so much more than a wife.

Our wedding was much better than a big fuss. It was a party we invited ourselves to along with friends and family. The next day we went to Greece for a two-week honeymoon – I'm smiling now, thinking of it.

A warm Mediterranean afternoon, napping in a cheap room on a beach, listening to the buzz of Vespas outside. Weird, there's no Doppler effect. The Vespas aren't coming and going. With a start we realize, no Vespas. It's a huge bee racing around the room! Simultaneously we made the same shocked face, like Munch's The Scream. Later, we named it the Bee Face. Over 28 years we would make the Bee Face when we saw something we liked, something we were shocked at, to add meaning to a moment. It was part of our day-to-day life.

This memory is a bit of skin hanging on a barbed wire fence. I know it's forever gone, never to be repeated. Yet I still smile, thinking of Donna and us.

Lobsters, oh how you loved a lobster while we vacationed or for your birthday at the Palm. I would crack the claws for you. The smile, the yum on your face, was pure joy to see and to hold in my memories. Did I offer you enough lobsters during your 59 trips around the Sun?

I remember every moment. The peace and joy. Our pets. Our vacations. Especially the clowning around. Just our life. The you and I became we. There were vacations and there was work, and that was all we needed for thirty years, because ... we.

When you were sick, our cell phones went from being utilitarian objects to being art pieces. Home screens and ringtones mattered because we were using them so much more. I rarely gave my number out; it was mostly for employees and you, but you thought I should have a special, resonant ringtone for you. You picked the Psycho theme song.

Bee Face!

You'd send me emails when work was
light and you were in joyful vacation
mode. Something like this, just to let me
know that "all is good and fun":

Prada and Levis
and shopping on eBay
Facials and cashmere
and doing things MY way
A fast connection
and big diamond rings
These are a few of my favorite things

When the dogs bark,
when the job's due,
when I'm feeling sad

I simply remember my favorite things
and then I don't feeeeeeeeeel ... so bad.

ON THE CUSP

Thanksgiving of 2008, we spent at our place in Tribeca, celebrating America's annual food porn marathon with my sister and her partner and a few of our neighbors.

I was the cook in our two-person family, no different from most of my life. My mother and father both worked so I'd be tasked when I came home from school and start dinner or at the very least put something in the oven.

We were first-generation immigrants so meals were the definition of family. The kitchen and the dining room were the centerpiece of the home. It was not only the food that structured our lives, it was setting the table and using silverware correctly, fork in the left hand and knife in the right. Donna's childhood and food was not the same. In a small way I wanted to have our Sunday and holiday meals make up for what she missed.

Now in my two-person family, I cooked and Donna selected everything I used to cook with and serve on. Donna never saw the value in cooking when ordering in was so easy. If we were out at dinnertime and she got hungry, hypoglycemic, she'd eat anywhere. Me, I wanted to walk a few blocks to find something worthy of my palette.

"Nope! Here, now, don't screw with me," she'd say.

We could get loud in public at times.

> That Thanksgiving, I was well underway with cooking and then my sister showed up and jumped in with directions and suggestions, pushing me out of the way or making fun of my techniques, same as last year. It wouldn't be a holiday without her. And this Thanksgiving was no different. That was the natural order.

Donna was doing what Donna did best, setting the table and arranging everything in visual perfection—flowers, napkins, candles, and tablecloth, all color correct. Silverware placed carefully next to the dishes. Serving pieces laid out, ready to accept the bounty. Nothing left to chance.

That year she brought out the set of dishes that, when my mother passed, ended up with me. From the '50s, they were kind of The Jetsons meets Bauhaus. One problem, though: it was a place setting for four. Donna spent nearly a year searching online and bargaining on eBay to find additions to the set, including a one-of-a-kind lemonade pitcher. In the end she built a complete setting for eight.

For the past two years Donna had been working at an ad agency on 42nd Street. She couldn't take cabs to and from work—downtown was prohibitively expensive—so she became a straphanger.

One evening she came home and told me, "I was getting on the train and my foot fell between the train and the platform, up to my knee. Two riders lifted me up."

She was nonchalant about it but I could imagine the train taking her leg off too well, or even dragging her down the platform and smashing her into a wall. What would I do if anything happened to her?

The day after Thanksgiving we started Christmas. We bought our small tree down the block, put it up on the trunk in the hallway that connected the dining room to the back room, and decorated it immediately.

Many of the decorations were from my childhood. Very few were recent purchases, though Donna added to our collection in her own style. Our neighborhood had a number of three- and four-star restaurants that always decorated their storefronts with greenery, lights, and ornaments. Donna was struck by one particular restaurant whose ornaments were simple and gray. One day as she was walking our Westie, Nina, she grabbed one of their ornaments right off the railing. All I could say when she came home and showed me was, "Huh?"

"Power to the people," she replied.

She purloined a fair collection
of those over the years.

Donna and I weren't emotionally effusive,
we didn't do public displays of affection,
but something about Christmas turned
up the burners. Maybe it was the heat of
competition as we tried to outdo each other
with presents. Or, as the years progressed
and it was just us, Christmas became the
surrogate for the family we never had.

Our quiet, comfortable apartment took on
a shine, more light, more warmth. The usual
scrum of our day-to-day lives lifted and we
were more present in our world. And Donna
started to work on her cards.

Most of our friends and families had surrendered to email by now, or e-cards at the most. Donna refused. She sent paper cards by mail for anniversaries, birthdays, and Valentine's Day, but Christmas was her moment to shine. She would buy different boxes of cards, mostly from the Museum of Modern Art, and selected cards for each person meticulously. Then she would pen short notes in perfect art school lettering, finely honed over the years of doing comps and layouts.

It wasn't about single-handedly reviving
a tradition for her. She had a year of love
saved up for those few on her list and this
was how she could send it. She was private
but she was personal and if she valued you,
you knew it.

These holiday meals and cards were, for our
friends, little glimpses through a peephole of
our slow dance together, alone.

We could drive five hours to Maine, being silent most of the time, not out of disregard for each other, but basking in the fact we were there together. In our older truck we couldn't hear the radio over highway-speed wind but in our car, in later years, we'd lace our silence with music. Donna turned to me:

"What was that lyric?" she asked.
"I didn't catch it."
"Well, what song is this?"
I sort of crinkled up my nose and squinted as if I were listening carefully. "No idea."
"Who was the group?"

Silence.

"You know you haven't recognized any song in about three hours? Bug," she grinned, "you might really be brain-damaged."

I got her back for that one. The last car had a satellite radio and when a song started playing, the band's name and song title would stream across the display. Donna didn't notice that at first so I bet her $50 that I could get the next two songs. I did. She was impressed. Then she was pissed when she figured it out.

I don't remember the genesis of "Bug" but the feeling was always there: I was a cute Bug to her. Sometimes she called me Zander for no reason. Her nickname was Mandy Jane, also out of nowhere. It seemed to fit with Zander. We just had a meandering stream of playfulness and whimsy through 30 years. It was our secret, like her tea sandwiches.

Donna hated the food along 42nd Street. Everything was expensive and catered to middle-aged middle-management. When she had worked downtown, the food selection was broad and varied; she could always run out and grab a slice or a sandwich and work at her desk.

She wasn't thrilled about this job, though she appreciated having one. I began to make her lunches a few days a week, hoping it would help. Each evening while the TV was on, I'd dig through the fridge for fresh turkey, lettuce, tomato, mayo, and whole-grain bread. Then I'd put just the right amount of mayo for her on each slice of bread, build the sandwich with perfect balance, and cut it in half diagonally because that just looked better to her. Sometimes I'd cut off the crust and quarter it—she'd call those her "little tea sandwiches."

Then I'd carefully wrap the sandwich in wax paper and tape the edges, place it deliberately in a plain brown paper bag with her name lettered on the outside, and add a cookie or two on top. Some mornings I'd fill one of her stainless steel thermoses with a homemade latte.

> I miss doing those little things
> for her as much as I miss her.

Wrapping those sandwiches, I was imitating Donna wrapping presents. (Besides, I'd hear about poorly folded corners.) Over December, her Christmas presents for friends and family—just me; her mother had died long ago, her brother just a few years back—appeared under our tree. Every wrapping was homemade, sometimes illustrated by hand, a lifetime of graphic design applied to each one. She'd make them works of art like they were on commission, matching bows to paper, paper to person, packaged with precision. I'd sit in the living room and glance at her pouring herself out to us through craft paper and ribbons, then peek at the ones under the tree, wondering what she'd found for me.

> Some years we spoiled each other. Other years, not so much, with the expected ebb and flow of a marriage. I had a feeling about this year, though. She was going to present some fierce competition for me. I needed to up my game.

My favorite presents she gave straight to the boy in me. Slinkies, Tin Tin adventures, Gumby and Pokey figures, tiny books about love and jokes, the dancing bugs "for Bug" one year; she tailored every item to a part of me. What had she seen in me this year?

She coughed again across the room,
elbow-deep in wrapping paper.

"I think this is bronchitis," she griped.
"It won't go away. I'm calling the doctor again."

"He'll just try another medication."
Two, so far.

This time he asked her to come in so he
could have an X-ray done in his office.
There were three small, dark areas on
her lungs. He scheduled a PET scan for
December 29.

On December 26th, we had tickets to see South Pacific at Lincoln Theater. This was unusual for us. It was to be a fun evening at the theater but my mind was reeling, circling back to that coming PET scan. Her own fear, never mentioned, was palpable nonetheless, as I sat next to her in the cramped seats in the dark, trying to find lightness and light in a musical about love on a far away island paradise. I never heard the song "Happy Talk" that evening. I was somewhere else.

We had two weeks left of December. It wasn't Christmas anymore. It was a slow walk into a La Brea tar pit. Denial was a quiet feeling. So was hope. Fear was a loud brass cymbal stuck in my throat.

December 29th, we hopped into a cab and went to the diagnostic center near Union Square. The buzzer was outside; there was no doorman. Opposite the entrance was a large freight elevator finished in cold, utilitarian stainless steel. I imagined I heard my heartbeat echoing in that cavernous steel chamber during the two-story ride down.

> The doors opened to a waiting room and a reception desk. It was starkly lit with fluorescent lighting, and everyone waiting had sallow faces. Was it the lights, or illness? No one sits in this basement because they're healthy.

Donna and I checked in, giving the receptionist her health insurance card, Social Security number, and other information. We signed the check-in sheet and took seats.

The chairs were comfortable and set in rows, back to back. There was a flat-screen TV on the wall with some daytime show on. We were lost in our thoughts. Not much was said. Not much could be said.

We visited the diagnostic center from December 2008 until June 2011; I would guess ten times. Each time it was the same but one of those waits stayed with me. That day the TV was airing The Rachael Ray Show. Ray was making hamburgers and said the secret to a juicy hamburger is to finely grate an onion so it produces liquid, then fold that liquid into the ground meat. I tried it later and it worked. I do that to this day and every time I do, I'm sitting in that waiting room, waiting for Donna to return so we can get the hell out of there.

That Christmas while walking in Soho we found a store that had a yellow-and-black plaid down parka, to protect her from the cold.

I hate that coat. It failed. I failed.
Nothing could protect her.

It's still hanging in our bedroom closet.

DIAGNOSIS

Donna came home from work. I was preparing dinner.
She said, "We need to talk."

                      It was two days after her PET scan.
                      I sat in the butterfly chair. She sat
                      on the lime green ottoman, recently
                      purchased to brighten the room.

"Dr. S. called and left a voicemail at work. He said
I have Stage IV cancer and six months to live."

We sat there, silent, looking at each other. Donna began to cry. In the thirty years I'd known her that had never happened.

When she spoke again, she spoke slowly. "I don't want to go through treatment or die a painful death. Let's move to Oregon so I can be put down on my terms. I will leave you everything."

It was that simple for her:
her death managed her way
on her terms and timeline.

The life we had sought and shared was over.
We'd been evicted and the building torn
down. It felt like opening a well-loved book
and finding all the letters jumbled, the logic
and meaning gone. You'll never read that
again, Mandy Jane, Bug. Here's a game of
Boggle, that's your life now.

Dr. S. was our primary care physician. He got us in to see Dr. B., head of oncology at a teaching hospital, that week. Before Dr. B. pulled out her chart Donna asked, "Am I going to die in six months?"

"Well, not so fast. Let's take a look."

He did a physical, reviewed her charts and films. Then he looked her in the eye and touched her hand.

"Your tumors are small but inoperable. The tumor in the brain is not absorbing much contrast, which is good. You are asymptomatic and healthy. So six months is not the plan, but this is Stage IV and we'll do the best we can."

He placed a blank sheet of paper on the desk and drew a horizontal line on it. Over the left end, he wrote "Dr. B." Over the right, he wrote "Donna."

"Donna, make a check on this line for how you want us to work together. On the left, I make all the decisions based on the best evidence, my experience, and your disease. On the right, you make all the decisions and I will follow that."

Donna checked the middle of the line.

In that hour with Dr. B. we put Oregon on hold. He believed in her and he gave us hope.

That was the moment Donna gave me her cancer. She turned it over to me. This was not an exercise in denial or an abdication from life. It was her way of finding her dignity so she could continue to work and live without being annoyed by the cancer. She wasn't fighting the cancer. She was having it trafficked like a job jacket for a 12-page sales aid. "Bring me the job jacket when I need to meet a due date or review it or make a decision. Otherwise, don't bother me with it."

Her job was managing her life, whatever might be left of it. My job was logistics and details.

I was with her for every visit to Dr. B. Over time that room with its two straight-back chrome-and-black chairs, the small desk, the light box, and exam table became an oasis of hope. It was where Donna's death march was momentarily halted by treatments and, most of all, by Dr. B. placing her in the center of his clinical world. He knew what she needed clinically and what we both needed emotionally.

We respected him but we drove
the conversations, since neither of
us was shy or afraid of physicians.
Sometimes I'd speak over Donna.

"Excuse me," she'd say, glaring.

Dr. B. got a kick out of it every time. That was the woman I married, complete control and power. She made all her medical decisions for two years.

In the first visit with Dr. B., he said the first and most important need was to remove the brain tumor. There were no symptoms from that tumor, though I noted that Donna would sometimes put things away in the kitchen in odd places. I'd find boxes of dried pasta in the fridge or pantry items with canned goods. Nothing outlandish, just not her. Dr. B. recommended a neurosurgeon who was willing to do the surgery and was highly regarded. Dr. B. set an appointment with Dr. RS. the next week.

The appointment with Dr. RS. was at Dr. B.'s office. Donna and I sat quietly in the exam room, waiting, not knowing what to expect. Some guy was going to enter the room. He was the guy who was going to poke and prod her brain from the inside.

The door opened. Standing there was this 6-foot-plus man of Indian descent. He did not have a lab coat on, wearing instead a grey suit, a blue shirt, a perfectly matched silk tie of the right width, and highly polished black shoes. I would guess the suit was a $3,000 Ermenegildo Zegna. His hair was on the short side but well groomed and his nails were perfectly shaped.

> He introduced himself and spoke directly to Donna, softly, deliberately, and slowly explaining what her status was, what he was going to do, and how he believed he would be successful. He showed us the PET scan of her brain and tumor. There at the center of her being was an invader, an alien, intent on changing her reality. And this confident, skilled, impeccably dressed, tall, soft-spoken man was going to slay that alien.

Donna asked a few questions, her comfort with Dr. RS. pooling around her shoulders like a warm scarf. On the cab ride home she said, "He has the style and presence of someone I can trust. He is the Don Draper of neurosurgeons."

I was relieved because Donna's instincts were always finely tuned and rarely failed her.

On February 6th, 2009, we woke up at 5 a.m. and hopped a cab to St. Luke's-Roosevelt for Donna's craniotomy. A nurse at Intake, going down a checklist, asked Donna what she'd ingested over the last twelve hours. Donna said she had a latte at 5 a.m.

"You had a latte? We can't admit you."

It was my fault. I misread the pre-surgical instructions and let her have the latte. #EpicFail.

Donna ripped me a new one, brutally, in front of the anesthesiologist and anyone else within fifty feet. She had an appointment. She was ready. She had never missed a due date for work and here she was entrusting me to make this happen. Her brain was the single most important organ in her body. It took all her courage to do this, to be ready to have her brain cut into. And because of me she would have to start all over again. Her a-hole husband had fucked up.

> The anesthesiologist watched us,
> fearing for my life. He knew Donna
> had gathered every ounce of strength
> just to get here and now it was being
> sapped because of me.

> > "I'll admit you," he said.
> > "We'll all lie about the latte."

With that, we were a team again. I retained my job as a caregiver, but the bar was raised. I had to do better. Be more accurate, be more present, be secondary to her threatened life. It was really a gift Donna gave me, her cancer, and I needed to cherish that.

Donna went to change into a surgical gown. She lay down on a gurney and was brought out. I walked with her while she was being transported up to the surgical unit. On the surgery floor, Dr. RS. came out and spoke to us. The perfect suit was exchanged for pressed green surgical scrubs and a cap. He spoke directly to Donna, all the while touching her hand. Donna asked about her hair.

"Will you have to shave my head?"
He said, "Let's see what I can do."

A week later, after the bandages were removed, her hair was there and it was nearly impossible to find a scar.

Years later, following Donna's death, I sent an email to Dr. RS. telling him she had passed. To my surprise, he wrote back.

Hi Mark

Thank you for your email. I am so sorry to hear about Donna. You certainly have my condolences. I am comforted that she was able to do so well for so long.

I think that you did an amazing job in supporting her and taking care of her. Ultimately that was the most important thing for her and more impactful than any surgery or chemotherapy.

I am always inspired by patients like Donna and the strength and dignity with which they approach life given their circumstances. I believe that theirs is a deeper, more profound existence than we may ever know.

Please know that I am happy to help in any way that I can. Take care.

Three years later, I learned Dr. RS. had moved from St. Luke's-Roosevelt to Mount Sinai. A neighbor of mine is an anesthesiologist there. Riding up the elevator in our apartment building, I asked if he ever ran across Dr. RS. He said yes.

> "Would you say hi to Dr. RS. for me? You may need to remind him that I was Donna's husband and he did her craniotomy in 2009."

A day or two later my neighbor said he spoke with Dr. RS. and he did indeed remember Donna and me, without prompting. Dr. RS. told my neighbor that he had performed the surgery because no one was giving Donna any hope and that was his goal: to give her hope when she had none.

Following the surgery, Donna went into recovery. My sister was with me and we sat and waited for her to be moved to the neurosurgical ICU unit. I could not stop thinking about her possible death and what we were going to face. I blamed myself for it. With no rational thought for why, I just did. My guilt was the cloak I wrapped around her to protect her. This had to fall on me and not her.

Once she was in the ICU, I was allowed to see her. The ICU was not a separate room. It looked like a tech startup. The open architecture showed small glass partitions between beds—some occupied, some empty—with machines beeping a syncopated cadence. The lighting was dimmed. There was Donna in a bed, her head bandaged, drifting in and out of a morphine-induced state of unconsciousness.

Those two days in the ICU were the most brutal time we'd ever shared. That first night at around midnight, I left the hospital and hailed a cab in the bitter cold. I got in and sat in the darkness of the backseat, emotionally spinning out of control. I suddenly burst out to the cabdriver about my wife being in the hospital with stage IV cancer, and how I was afraid. Here I was, sharing with a stranger I would never see again, "My wife is dying."

The driver was kind. He told me about his wife's cancer and how she was admitted to Calvary Hospice in the Bronx and how well they cared for her. I'm not sure I was comforted.

Late the second evening, my friend K came to the ICU to support me. Donna was awake and bitter. How could I allow anyone to see her in that condition? And why her, why that friend? After K left and all the next day, Donna did not stop reminding me how I'd failed her. How I didn't take her to Paris enough. How I wasn't the best husband. What I didn't do. The cloak of guilt was working overtime. She was angry and she was alive.

For the next two and a half years, I owned her disease. I missed one radiation appointment, one ENT appointment, and one ophthalmologist appointment, out of dozens. I packaged pills for her. I held her hand through every chemo infusion. The list is long and I wonder how much I was motivated by guilt as well as love, and gratitude that she trusted me.

I guess it doesn't matter. She died, I am alive.

Years later I read C.S. Lewis's essay, "A Grief Observed."

> "To some I'm worse than an embarrassment. I am a death's head. Whenever I meet a happily married pair I can feel them both thinking. 'One or the other of us must some day be as he is now.'"

I was the docent for her death.

HAIR

Top of the list of Donna's fears was loss of her mind. Her brain was her drive, the center of her life. All she became, all she did, all she was, came from her mind. Her world of color, style, design, vision, and sense of balance resided there. But as mercurial as she was about her creativity, she was about her hair.

At the time the evidence seemed clear. After craniotomies, before chemotherapy, whole-brain radiation (WBR) reduced the incidence of secondary brain tumors and improved overall survival rates.

Dr. C., the radiation oncologist,
was the polar opposite of Dr. B.

"Guy looks like he's twelve years
old," I wanted to whisper to Donna.

He spoke briefly about the clinical evidence
for WBR and quickly moved to scheduling,
did a cursory exam, and reviewed her charts.
I attributed the clipboard approach to the
fact that radiation oncology is more about
the math and less about patient care.

"What about alopecia?" Donna asked.

"If I do this, will I lose my hair?
And if I do, will it grow back?"

>He was casual, off the cuff. "There'll be hair loss and it comes back in some cases." He went on about something else and I didn't push. I wanted her to have all the life she could.

For three weeks, five days a week, they radiated her brain. It slowed her down, especially in weeks two and three. She would schedule her radiation appointments for noon to 1:00. That would give her some time to sleep a bit, then we'd head to the radiation unit, grab lunch before or after, and return home. Donna would lie down and take a nap while I started dinner and worked on the details of closing my office or packing items for storage. After dinner we'd sit on the sofa and watch some TV. I'd turn to her and she'd be asleep.

    Her hair began to fall out in clumps.
    Then in May she started chemotherapy.

Donna
to Dr. C.

As per my conversations with you and your office, I should be expecting to see full hair regrowth beginning 3 months later, or by last week of June. (Nothing so far.) Please understand that I am very concerned with the possibility of permanent hair loss, as this was not something that was discussed prior to treatment. If I have been or am worried for nothing, please let me know.

Also, if you are at all able to send a couple of pictures from your files of post-treatment hair growth among your female patients (3 and 6+ months post)? That would really put my mind at ease. Don't worry, they won't end up on a blog and you can crop or blacken the faces. I only care about the hairline, thickness and overall coverage.

Dr. C.
to Donna

I know the hair issue is frustrating; believe me I understand. Unfortunately it's an unpredictable thing so I don't know when to expect it. I don't have any pictures but if I see patients in f/u I will ask their permission. I will also speak w/Dr. B. about the chemotherapy as this can also affect hair growth.

She was never crazy about her hair.
It was wavy or kinky, I guess; very Jewish.

> "I hate the smell of vinegar," she said once.
> "It's repulsive. My mother used to wash
> my head with it every week, trying to
> straighten my hair."

Throughout our 28 years her shampoos, conditioners, oils, and post-shampoo serums filled the shower caddy plus an entire shelf in the linen closet in our bedroom. The colorful bottles generally displayed French-sounding names with copy stating "evolution in hair treatment system" or "protects hair from breakage and enhances manageability."

But that was nothing compared to the combs and brushes. On her dresser was a silver tray that held no less than three brushes and four combs, made of different materials, with teeth of varying length and spacing. On our third Christmas I bought three more tortoise-shell combs from an antique store. Each one had wide spacing between the teeth. She was so touched by that gift.

> "You really do get me, don't you?
> That is so perfect."

Then there were the headbands, barrettes, and hairclips. The headbands were a vast array of colors, styles, widths, and materials. She didn't wear them daily; it was just her "Headband Period." Lift a lid of her large tin container like a popcorn pail and there were plaid, black, gray, red, brown, gingham headbands and more, like so many snakes curled up in a quiet sleep.

Donna
to Dr. C.

Re: hair loss and regrowth, the chemo regimen I've started is a newer combo with a less toxic profile. Dr. B. believes it to be "follicle friendly" (my expression, not his) so hair growth should not be affected, or affected by much. Again, while I am certainly concerned with "when," I am more concerned with "if," as we've discussed. "Full hair regrowth beginning at around 3 months" "will grow in thicker than before" (as per your assistant) were claims I took to heart, and in fact influenced my decision to proceed with WBRT to begin with, as compared to other options.

Our home was five blocks north of the World Trade Center. The morning of 9/11, I was already at my office, one block closer to the towers. Donna was getting into a cab to head to her job on 21st Street when the second plane struck. By the afternoon all businesses were closed. No trains were running; no cabs could be hailed. The power went out just after Donna started walking home. My cell had died and so did our house landline. We were out of touch.

She got home about 4 or 5 p.m. but the NYPD had placed blue wooden barricades below Canal Street and no one could enter Tribeca, even residents. I had brought my employees back to the apartment but they had all left to find their ways home. Then Donna walked in.

> "How the hell did you get past the Canal Street barricades?"

> "I walked the line till I found one with only one cop, and when he wasn't looking I ducked under and ran like hell."

I gaped at her. And noticed that she was
wearing a bandanna that hadn't been there
that morning. It was camouflage, too, which
Donna did not consider a color found in
nature and definitely not fashion. I pointed
at it and turned my head slightly as if to say,

"Huh?"

In the most matter-of-fact way she said,
"We're at war."

She'd bought it to cover her face from the dust.
It became her scarf during all the months we
stayed in our grim home for the cleanup. She
put two small American flags on our door.

Donna
to Dr. C.

    I wanted to let you know that the alopecia on top of my head remains unresolved. I remain deeply disappointed that this end result is so radically different from what was discussed with me prior to treatment. Overall, between that and your staff's (M specifically) surly incompetence, I question if remaining under your care is in my best interest. Although I do not want to switch physicians at this point, I'm sure that you can understand my concerns.

She tried to stay positive throughout the loss of her hair, wearing bandannas and hats and searching the Internet to find solutions. Aside from that email she didn't express her fear, anger, or depression, but they were palpable.

I hadn't understood. She was less annoyed by her hair and more… working with the tools she was given. So she didn't have a blank canvas, all right. Her curls became her brush and paints to complete her image of herself. They were her brainwaves, her way of making an impact, like a graphic artist uses type and white space. When you took in her person and presence, your eye fell on her hair first and last, and she knew it. As she changed it to match her styles over the years—some angst when she didn't like it, full pride when she did—it housed her willpower. And as it dropped away, so did her sense of choice.

We spent weeks looking at wigs.

"Too phony," she'd say. "Too Sheitel."

> (The wig married Orthodox Jewish women wear.)

None of the options were enough.
My heart was breaking for her.

Finally, she found someone who matched
extensions to her hair and cut them in a
style she could live with, but the devastation
to her heart and spirit had been done.

One day she said, "My mother had breast cancer when I was a teenager. All her hair fell out."

This wasn't a new revelation. Donna told me about it when we were dating. But I had never realized that what her mother went through made such a profound impact on her. Now Donna wasn't just afraid of losing her style and her life. She was being pulled back into a childhood that she had always firmly shoved into silent history. The past she'd shunned was circling back to today.

> If I'd only realized it earlier—but I don't know what I would have done. I should have pushed Dr. C. harder.

In the middle of year two, we were at a restaurant and WBR came up. Suddenly we were arguing about it, heated, loud, and angry.

"It was survival!" I snapped.

"It was intractable alopecia and a radiation oncologist who lied," she snapped back. "It broke me."

A woman and her son sitting at the next table stared at us. We just went in harder.

"It saved you. At any cost, anything, I want you alive!"
"It's supposed to be about what I want, and what I want is quality of life! You were supposed to handle the doctors!"

I started to use my words, the four-letter ones.
"Watch your mouth!" said the woman nearby.

I turned on her. "You are in New York City. Your son goes to school here, he knows these words."

Then I turned back to Donna, feeling guilty about attacking that lady for all of thirty seconds.

Donna said, "I would rather be dead than look like a freak."

The fight was over. #Dropthemic.

I let the world form an opinion of Donna based not on her self-image but mine. I wanted the world to see her alive and all she wanted was to be whole.

MEMORIES

"There's a reason they call it history.
It happened then."

Donna saw no reason to talk about the past. It was done, over and gone, all stacked in an abandoned room. She wasn't denying her past, but affirming that her life was here, now, and better.

We only spoke about her childhood when she dropped a snippet to make a point. "I like kasha. It's comfort food for me." That was my cue to make it part of a meal. The rest (maybe "my mother was a terrible cook") was unimportant or unnecessary.

Four years after her death and eight years after her brother Jack's, an envelope appeared in our mailbox, handwritten, addressed to Donna from Berkeley. It was from a friend of Jack's last girlfriend, Brenda. Brenda had died and this friend was cleaning old boxes out of her basement. He'd found a carton of photos and documents from Donna and Jack's childhood.

Would Donna like them?

A couple of weeks later the box arrived. It was beat up and taped haphazardly, like it was shouting, "All yours, good luck!" I placed it on the stainless steel kitchen island, wondering, why bother? Do I want to see what's inside? Donna didn't. She had exerted control over her world precisely by shunning this stuff. That's how it ended up across the country. Would any of it add to my memories? Do I care? WTF?

Inside this battered brown box were photos of Donna. Standing in our kitchen, I picked up faded pictures of a little girl at a birthday party, a little girl with a brother, a little girl with her grandparents, a little girl posing, a little girl with her dad.

They were just images, standing alone. Without her voice and memory, they were mute. What is a photograph without the story behind it? If Donna were here, would she have shared memories as she looked at these, told me more, given me the context I longed for?

Each photo felt like a piece of a jigsaw puzzle. I had no reference, no box-cover. I held each photo carefully by the edge and rotated it slowly, savoring each angle to see more clearly the person and place in each.

I knew her for thirty years. Maybe I could reverse engineer the thirty before we met. Maybe I could guess my way into discovering more about her.

I kept putting the box away and pulling it back out, trying to complete a picture and finish a memory. Over each photo I'd drift off, imagining her voice adding a caption.

"That was in Orange, my second
birthday party. It was just Mom, Dad,
Jack, and my grandparents."

> "My parents took us to the Catskills for
> a week during the summer. Oy vey. I
> learned to ride a horse there."

I study the face, the clothes, the place in each photo. I see little girl Donna at a birthday party, sitting in front of a cake with candles, looking so happy. She's really posing there. Look at that posture, her stare, as a child. Fuck you, this is me. Look at me.

I remember her saying once, "When I was three I would dress myself in the clothes I wanted, which pissed Helen off." Helen was her mother. "I demanded that I go shopping with her to select my clothes."

        I imagine she styled herself and her pose for every photograph, exactly the way she wanted. I recognize the woman I married in that. Her palette then was not as rich but you can see the spark.

I understand that I want to see her strength then so I can believe it was always there.

I see vulnerability in the photos too, and a sense of wonder. Her smile in the pictures with her father, she only showed that smile when she was safe. It's clear he doted on her. When she mentioned any warm, happy memory from her childhood, he was usually in it.

He died when she was ten. Helen raised two children alone, a single woman in the late '50s and '60s. She worked her ass off to support them. Jack, the oldest child and only male in a Jewish family, was the apple kugel of her eye. While she worked, Jack was the authority at home after school.

Suddenly, I remember. Donna let it slip once. "He locked me in a closet so I wouldn't annoy his reading."

She never mentioned it again. I wanted to comfort her but it was history. She would have seen my response to her past as illogical.

> Life's jigsaw cut Donna into pieces, yet the woman I met and fell in love with was a completed person, no assembly required by the world or by me. No stitches or seams or staples or nails, she was totally Donna. All you saw was a smooth, polished surface.

And somehow she'd perfected her self-assembly by high school. One day in the car, we were listening to a Grateful Dead concert recorded at the Fillmore East. I off-handedly said, "That would have been so cool to go to."

> Donna said, "I was there. I sold pot to the cheerleaders for the ticket money and snuck out of the house and went. You are such a wimp."

>> I laughed. I was less of a wimp and more of an obedient son.

I know she'd asked Helen about college.
Donna did well in school, was very smart,
and wanted to be an educated woman.

> Helen replied, "Your brother is a genius and
> I need to pay for his education so he can
> help us. Jack will become a doctor and save
> the family. You are a girl so you don't need
> college because you'll get married."

So she left. Donna from day one, split
and soldered back together, left with all
the pieces of her in place.

An art director far beyond her career, Donna cut chance out of her life. Everything she touched, she centered, perfectly spaced and well designed. She told me that during high school, at the height of the anti-war movement, she was the poster and sign maker. I wish those could have been in the box. I would love to have seen them. Later, putting herself through college, she was an illustrator.

> "I could draw plaid," she told me,
> and then proved it.

Art, graphic design, illustration are not haphazard. They don't just happen. You start with a blank piece of paper, then follow the logic of where things go, where color exists, and how they play together. She was a master at filling a void with meaning and creating memories for others.

Eventually she rebuilt a kind of fractured connection with her mother and brother, but New Jersey: never again. Born, raised, gone.

"I spent my whole life trying to get out of there and I'm not about to go back."

But she didn't need to be in New Jersey to be New Jersey. She was fierce, she took no prisoners, and she didn't tolerate fools. And nothing was left to chance. Meeting me might have been one of her only accidents. Well, meeting me, and her hair.

I tried to make our family of two her family for life. I'll never know if I succeeded.

IN THE GARDEN
OF TREATMENT

May 7th, 2009, was Donna's first chemotherapy treatment. She needed to take steroids as part of the prep; the dosage increased as the day for infusion approached and tapered off afterwards. In all she was taking steroids for five days during this first round of chemo.

While we watched TV at night, I made packets of the different dosages. I sat on the floor at the glass coffee table with the bottle of pills and a pill cutter. In front of me were small brown envelopes and a pen. I would cut the pills or put two of the full dose in an envelope. I picked up a pen and marked the day on which to take them. Every date was my apology to her for letting this happen.

In the first round, she had nausea and some vomiting. She didn't throw up her shoes; it was just annoying for her and sad for me. I was working a part-time consulting gig; the rest of each week was full of appointments for tests, scans, and chemo.

The infusion room was on the same floor at Dr. B's office. It was a large room full of light from the windows facing a park and the classic assorted skyline of buildings and offices. Fifteen infusion chairs were arrayed around the room, with a regular chair beside each. The infusion chairs were actually recliners, since it's important to be comfortable when you're being poisoned. Looming over the recliners were stainless steel stands on spindly legs. They held the chemicals in clear bags as a computerized pump pushed the fluids down to the needles. Most bags held clear fluid; others had various colors. The stands and bags looked like the staff had sculpted them as totems or prayers for life. We were sitting in a sculpture garden, contemplating.

Around us were people in various states of age and health. Some were curled up under blankets, trying to rest or escape where they were and why. Their faces were drawn and exhausted from the passive submission to the aggressive treatment. Sometimes they were gaunt. Others were talking quietly with family and friends or doing their best to engage with the nurses and physicians who attended to the pumps and bags. I saw crossword puzzles, books, headphones and mp3 players, and one person knitting, her wool draped over her recliner. Kind of like a subway car: "Next stop … Transfer to …" But we were stranded on a desert island, working together to be saved or, sometimes, giving up like Lord of the Flies.

Every now and then someone in a recliner would speak to another, "What are you here for?" We were all here for the same thing: to find life within our lives.

The standard first-line treatment shrank Donna's three lung tumors. One of them nearly resolved.

> All three returned. Dr. B. adjusted her treatment to the next line of intensity. We saw similar success but with shorter duration.

Over the next two years I witnessed the slow erosion of her life, my life, our life. During that first round of chemo she could only eat chicken soup so we'd go to Chinatown, walking there at first, eventually taking cabs. Her go-to dish was chicken dumpling soup. On weekends I would make a large pot of chicken noodle soup so she could heat it up during the day and for dinner.

With the second round, she could eat more. Since my office was near our apartment I would come home and start a meal.

> Once she said, "Remember before the diagnosis, when I'd come home and you'd be sitting and watching the news?"
>
> "Yeah. Business was in a down cycle."
> "You wouldn't engage with me. It hurt me."

I didn't defend, didn't hide. I just thought get out of my ass. My business sucked! I was on the verge of going belly up with a huge lease hanging over my head. Why are you doing this now? I just want to forget. I tried to focus, to understand what she needed out of this. Maybe she just needed me to hurt with her.

After dinner we'd clean up, do some chores, and put on the TV. We shared similar tastes to a point, and it was a good overlap. The one show Donna was most addicted to was Sons of Anarchy, featuring Kurt Sutter as Jax Teller. She loved the spelling J A X. It was her, all about communication. It premiered September of 2008. Those winter evenings, she'd burrow under an electric blanket, turn to me right before the show started, and say, "Jax is coming on. I do not want to hear a peep out of you for the next hour." She was not dead yet.

Saturdays were movie night and we'd walk over to the Battery Park City cinema, though walking was a chore. During the movie we shared a small popcorn. Well, I thought we shared it. She never had a chance, coming between me and popcorn.

The theater would darken and the trailers appear, and they stabbed me in the heart every time. That damn smooth voice telling us the plot of a film coming soon—would it be soon enough? Would Donna be here to see it? You know what's coming? Pain. More chemo, more fear, more gnawing of grief on my heart, soul, and memories. I lost hope every Saturday night before the feature even started. Donna never noticed. Or at least, if she did, she didn't say a word. Was it her denial or her respect for me? My mental reel wouldn't shut up: our movie was not going to have a happy ending.

But those nights always did. After the film we'd get home by 10:30 or so and then it was time to take Nina out. Our first Westie had been Willy and he was my dog or, more to the point, he was the dog for me—a big lug who wanted nothing more than to chase skateboards and look adorable. Nina, our second, was Donna's joy and love and eager recipient of hugs, kisses, and treats. As lovely as Donna, Nina was always freshly groomed with a traditional Westie cut. Nina was an art installation.

When we got home from the movies Donna would wait downstairs and I'd get Nina, who had quickly learned the routine. The second the elevator opened on the ground floor, she rushed at the glass doors, scratching like crazy to get out to see Donna. Donna would bend down and Nina would kiss the hell out of her face and bark. We'd stroll around the neighborhood then take her upstairs, give her bedtime biscuits, and end our date night on a better note than it started, at least for me.

About two months after her death I went to my first movie alone. I bought my popcorn and I remembered to grab napkins. She always made me go back when I forgot. The trailers came on and I sat there, lost and broken.

The first summer with chemo, Donna joined a gym for the first time in her life and began going on a daily basis, dressed in new gear and sneakers, carrying her water bottle. No, she was not power-lifting or doing an hour on a Step Master. This was not a "cancer-fighter beating cancer" walk-a-thon. She'd do what she could and how she could, and she was so proud of her efforts when I came home. I was elated as well but I would try to nudge her into doing more. Now, looking back, I see that I should have just expressed more joy for her.

    Around this time she also said she wanted to get a bike. I don't think she had ever made it past a tricycle—this was one of the photos I found in that box later, too late. She would have liked that expression on her face.

    I'd been riding bikes forever so I agreed to teach her to ride; now all we needed was the right bike.

My sister's partner had points from the company she worked for and she gave them to Donna to buy a bike. Donna spent two weeks finding just the right ride in the right color and style. We had a bike rack for our apartment shipped from Japan and I put that and the bike together. Then, per Donna's instructions, I tricked out the bike with chrome fenders, a wicker basket, and a bell. A pretty bell. A loud bell.

One Sunday we walked her bike over to a local pocket park with fairly calm streets. I was scared to death of a fall. Of course, she had a helmet but with chemo going on and the disease, I worried she would break something.

Instead, it was the usual husband-and-wife-learning-to-drive scenario with all the associated tension and raised voices.

> "Okay, go slow, don't turn the wheel too hard … Slow down, SLOW DOWN. Be careful, there's a car coming! Stop, stop! Don't you know how to stop?"
>
> > "Shut the fuck up, you're making me nervous. Let me do this, okay?!"

Somehow we finished and she did great. She wasn't the most confident or fluid but she was ready for the Hudson River Bike Path. We never went far, just enough for her to feel she did something she hadn't done before. Now I think she was more afraid and tired than she would admit. I was, too.

A few days a week we'd get the bikes down from the rack and Donna would put water, yogurt, napkins, and spoons in her basket. Then we'd merge into traffic and ride to the path, or walk if traffic was heavy. We'd ride north to a small area with tables and chairs just north of Stuyvesant High School. We'd sit and look at the Hudson River and New Jersey, and just hold hands and quietly think about tomorrow. She would eat the yogurt. And then we'd head back, Donna plinking her bell the whole way to warn everybody she was a bit nervous riding.

My consulting gig was in Jersey City, in an office that looked out over the Hudson into lower Manhattan. One morning my phone buzzed with a text from Donna. She'd sent a picture of an empty yogurt container with a plastic spoon on a table, facing the building I was in. She was one hell of an art director. My heart leaped. How did she do that ride herself with the traffic?

I remembered that when Donna left her job, she just walked out of the office the day before her craniotomy without a word to anyone about what was going on. She didn't take a box of stuff from her desk and her cubby was intact, as if she were leaving for vacation. Now she was finding new challenges to master and between the weakness and nausea and emotional trauma of chemo, this was a big one for her.

My phone buzzed again, another text.
"Are you proud of me?"

Fucking skippy I was.

ROUNDING THE CORNER

Ward III was new to the block and part of that hipster whiskey-cocktail bar trend. Previously that space was another bar that failed quickly and before that, a copy shop. This new bar was more welcoming to the neighborhood than trendy spots usually are, so sometimes I'd go in alone.

Being on the first floor of a five-story walkup on the south side of the street, it was a dim space with no natural light. The interior walls were dark oak, the bar was oak, the tin ceiling was painted dark brown, and behind the bar shelves of bottles climbed nearly to the 14-foot ceiling. Two Singer sewing machine tables, also oak, held bottles as well. I'd sit and order a beer and look at them, remembering living with my parents in my grandmother's tenement where she had the same machine and table.

They carried over seventy different whiskies, scotches, and bourbons. The bartenders were the owners and they had an encyclopedic knowledge of whiskey and cocktails. Ask about a liquor, and they would describe it in such great detail that it verged on lyrical storytelling. You could say just "sweet" or "spicy" and they'd tailor a cocktail for you.

Finally, I was part of something that wasn't caregiving. The owners didn't know about my infinite mental loop, the story with an unhappy ending every time. I didn't go often and I wouldn't stay long before the feeling that something would happen to Donna would gnaw on me, and the guilt for escaping her cancer welled up. I never doubted they would jump to help me if I asked, and never will.

December 31, 2010, Ward III threw an invite-only party, and the owners invited us. Donna and I wandered over and sat. I could see on her face she was in pain and wondering if this would be her last New Year's Eve. I was wondering, too. We would have sunk ourselves with that thought if the Ward III owners and general manager hadn't interrupted their busy night, often, to give Donna attention and love. She had put on some lipstick and makeup; she also tried to put on a happy face. It didn't fit and shards of darkness slipped from behind the mask. We made it to midnight, kissed, and went home. 2011 was beginning and it felt like the end already.

Her growing tumors had caused hypertrophic osteoarthropathy, an expansion of the long bones that also made her joints swell. Suddenly Donna couldn't walk or grip items without pain. It was a progressive condition and NSAIDs—aspirin, Advil, Aleve—provided some relief but not enough.

She carried her pain silently. Her best friend Joe told me recently that he met her for lunch at Ward III one day during this period; when he arrived at the bar Donna was already seated. She looked strong, beautiful, as perfectly put-together as ever, and was her usual bright, engaged self through lunch. Then they stood up to leave. Donna grimaced. She could barely stand and she limped as she walked. Joe didn't ask and she didn't complain. He simply helped her walk her four doors down to our building, crushed by her frailty and pain.

A new habit appeared in my routine. Going to and from work in Jersey City, I used my short commute to make my daily and weekly to-do lists. Instead of going straight upstairs, though, I'd sit on the recessed bench outside our building, afraid of what I'd find when I walked through our door. Would she be crying or in pain? Had she spent the day thinking of her death? I would just sit on the stoop in fear, until I'd realize how much I was thinking about myself as she was upstairs dying. Then I'd lift myself off the stoop and go upstairs to start dinner, resolved to reinforce whatever hope and joy she had.

> I was always surprised when I'd walk in. She'd be shopping online or doing a little consulting work of her own, thrilled to show me the paying work she'd done or the little happiness she'd bought.

By May the NSAIDs weren't working at all well,
and the pain in her knees and hands was worsening.

> "We can't do much about it," Dr. B. said. "It's
> a result of disease progression. There's a third
> line of treatment we can try on the tumors."

>> This was a bi-weekly treatment
>> and as with the others, the goal
>> was to shrink the tumors to
>> achieve some real pain relief.

We had a trip to Maine scheduled for mid-June.
Many years ago Donna had found a small cottage
in the town of Cape Elizabeth, not far from the
water. It was a beautiful two-bedroom home with
a magnificent, manicured yard and a series of small
English-style gardens, always bright with blooms of
color. We made the trip and spent a week sitting and
reading and watching Nina run around the yard.
A city dog never sees grass.

You couldn't tell Donna was dying in photographs. Her visual was not her reality. Or was it? Was her visual her own cancer-race victory?

We drove home to a CT appointment, supposed to determine if this third-line treatment was working. The pain was progressing, though, so any hope that the CT would show a change was left on the side of the road. After the scan the radiologist noted that Donna had pleural effusion, which is fluid surrounding the lungs. Dr. B. scheduled a thoracentesis to drain the fluid for July 11.

And so it goes.

The night before was Sunday. Instead of cooking dinner we went to the Odeon, a landmark in this neighborhood. It opened in the early '70s. By the mid '80s when we moved here, the old factory buildings around the neighborhood were largely empty or illegally converted, filled with artists and offering few if any services. Prior to us taking up residence in Tribeca The Odeon was virtually the only post-dancing, post-drinking, post-drugging, late-night carb oasis. Outside the brightly lit neon sign spelled ODEON in red; inside was an open room of tables in a French-bistro style. You'd walk in and see regulars: Andy Warhol, Basquiat, DeNiro, Belushi, and more. Leaving after dinner, you'd pass a stainless steel ticket dispenser about waist-high. When you pressed the handle a bright yellow ticket appeared that said Odeon in red type. That night I forgot to take one.

Donna could barely walk the two blocks to the restaurant. Coming home was worse.

The next morning I closed and locked our door while Donna leaned on a wall in the hallway. I carried her to a cab, watched from the cab as the city stretched and yawned in preparation for the day, and carried her through the hospital's emergency entrance. It was two years past the six months she'd been given to live.

"One day arm in arm
We left home and closed the door
You never returned"

HOSPICE

I held Donna's hand and watched her grimace as the doctor pushed the catheter through her back, into her lung. "This will work," I thought. "This will work, she'll be home soon."

Donna was admitted to the medical surgical unit. Her hospital room was a single, no roommate. The windows faced you as you entered and let in the daylight. Her bed was on the right, across from the bathroom.

After she was admitted and settled in her room, we sat for the day as residents, nurses, and Dr. B. came and went. She was showing more fear then I'd seen in the past. Her strength was declining.

At dinnertime I left to get Nina from boarding so I could feed and medicate her. When I got home I unlocked and opened our door without Donna beside me or inside.

The next day there was good news.
The thoracentesis had worked.

> Until it didn't. The fluid came back on
> Wednesday. I held her hand again, watched
> her face again, as another catheter stabbed
> her back. This time it worked. Until it didn't.

> "We need to discuss palliative care,"
> Dr. B. said.
>
> "Great," I thought, "this will give us,
> her, me, more time."

Normally there were two chairs in the room. Today it looked like a makeshift conference room with four additional chairs. They were perfectly arranged to project a sense of community and comfort. Dr. B. orchestrated where the chairs were placed, who sat, and who stood, thinking all the while of how this meeting would affect her. Palliative care was going to be a major change in her status. No longer was Donna living and being. She was Donna at the end of life.

The residents, social workers, and Hospice staff attending the meeting followed Dr. B.'s lead, staying focused on Donna the person, her life, and my status. Nobody was making the rounds with a clipboard.

Donna wasn't asking questions though. She wasn't engaged. Her eyes followed the chairs being moved and the white coats assembling and her shoulders slumped in surrender. It was the first time I'd ever seen her passive. "Don't give up," I thought. "Don't, please." I couldn't say it out loud because it would expose the obvious, that she was unable to rise and take flight from her bed.

The head of palliative care, Dr. E., took me aside. "The whole-brain radiation changed her brain," she said, "causing the delirium and agitation you see now. It's very similar to the changes from Alzheimer's." I tuned out, struggling to keep my emotions in check. When I tuned back in, she was saying, "Current standards of pain management in general medicine are not sufficient for end-of-life pain management due to tumor progression."

                              Not sufficient?

Dr. E. noted, "Palliative care physicians are better trained to manage this pain."

I returned to the room to sit next to Donna in her bed. Everyone was gone. The chairs were gone. She was silent. I was silent. I looked at her face and began to see what had been there for weeks. The sadness around her eyes was showing under her mask of fear.

I had my list of chores. I headed home and managed them. Feed Nina, walk Nina, make the bed, do the laundry, in the moment, no future, no past.

Wednesday, Thursday, Friday, I was with Donna seven to eight hours a day. Then I'd rush home, texting friends to visit Donna while I fed and walked Nina and gave her insulin injections.

Nina had to eat a pretty substantial meal prior to her insulin or her glucose would fall and she would suffer a seizure. Normally she wasn't a chowhound so I would sex up her food with some boiled chicken or steak, then stand over her and watch to make sure she ate it. Once she finished I filled a syringe, sat on the rug, and called her over. Gathering a skin fold on her neck, I injected the insulin. Nina and I had been dancing this waltz for two years now. I'd look at her and wonder if she understood what was happening. I wasn't sure I did; how could she?

Then we went out for a walk. Back home I'd check to see if it was going to rain and close the windows, make sure Nina had water, and turn on a small light. Donna would not leave Nina home in the dark no matter how many times I told her dogs have great eyesight.

While I was at home, a few times Donna called me from her hospital room. She was lost and agitated. The WBR that had kept her alive for me cost her hair, one of the two things she'd never wanted to lose. Now she was paying the price with her mind. I know she had wanted to die first.

> With Nina settled, I'd run for the number 4 or 5 train, get off at 14th Street, grab a slice, and head up to Donna's room.

Donna's best friend Joe came to visit her twice while she was in the medical surgical unit. During the first visit he said to me that Donna was distant and withdrawn. He could not easily engage with her, but she asked him to make sure he kept an eye on me after she died because she was worried about me.

> The next visit he mentioned to me, "She's wearing lipstick." She looked worse but she was remaining herself for her friends, staying positive.

But she was having trouble walking and eating. When I was there we just talked, held hands, and sometimes sat quietly. I would help her to the bathroom. During one of those walks of ten feet she had a bout of incontinence. I got her to the bathroom, cleaned her, and returned her to the bed. Then I hunted down latex gloves and cleaning supplies and wiped down the floor, properly disposing of the biohazard. I was ashamed that this woman who took no prisoners was surrendering to the disease without raising her hands. I was ashamed of my shame. Cleaning up was my apology to the universe for being me.

> Then Donna was put on risk for falls and could not get up to use the bathroom at all. The bedpan was her next step to the exit.

> I didn't get a copy of the marriage owner's manual. And if I did, I missed the entire section on preparing for death. WTF.

Dr. B. and Dr. S. suggested Home Hospice. When the Hospice intake staff spoke with me, they weren't wearing white coats. This was not clinical. It was business. The conversation felt like a sales call, done in a busy hallway of rushing physicians and nurses, with families of patients sitting nearby. Here I was, speaking and answering questions about Donna's death, in the most public of venues for the world to hear. Intake handed me papers to sign. I did not feel like a person about to lose his wife of 28 years, being offered hope and dignity. I felt like a transaction.

There is no blame here. I know I was an emotional wreck. I just wanted to say, "Do you get what I am going through?" Of course they did. Perhaps five times a day. How much hurt can you witness before it becomes a rote response?

The Home Hospice bed and other items were
ordered, delivered, and set up in our apartment,
with the bed in the living room. All the while I was
imagining Donna in the bed while I sat next to her,
catching up on the episode of Sons of Anarchy she
missed. I pushed out of my mind having to bathe
her, change her bedpan, attend to her pain meds, and
wake in the middle of the night to comfort her. None
of that was ever part of our plan thirty years ago but
I knew when the time came I'd face it like a Marine.
You do not leave your dead or wounded behind.
We would take that final march to the Medevac
helicopter that would carry her away.

Early that Saturday, Dr. S. spoke with me at the hospital. The floor was quiet and Dr. S. was at the nurse's station, looking at patient charts in thick, brightly colored plastic binders. He didn't really look up at me. Or maybe I don't remember because the numbness of it all was taking its toll.

He said, "Dr. B., the Hospice staff, and I think it would be best if Donna enters the Hospice unit in the hospital. The care she needs, even with medical aides, is beyond what Home Hospice can do."

I had been holding on to that trope of a wonderful, peaceful death at home, surrounded by friends and family circling her bed like supplicants kneeling to receive the communion of her life passing. Now I was hearing that even if she came home, she wouldn't have that. I wonder to this day if Dr. S. was straight with me, or if they all thought I was a caregiving failure and couldn't be trusted.

Monday, July 18, an orderly wheeled her bed out of the medical surgical unit while I walked alongside it. Donna turned on her side and went to sleep. We took the elevator down to the fourth floor and the Hospice unit, walked past rooms with the nearly dead lying motionless while loved ones stood next to the bed or sat in a chair nearby. Some spoke; all looked broken. In the family waiting area a few people were speaking quietly, while others just sat and stared. Unlike the medical surgical unit this wing had no beeping machines. No rushing of staff to administer meds, check on IVs, measure blood pressure, or prepare discharge instructions. No one was discharged here. They were released.

Donna stayed lucid even though the pain meds were increased. I was still a caregiver, not a pallbearer. I became a force of nature in the Hospice unit, scurrying back and forth to the nurses' station asking questions, speaking to nurses, social workers, patient aides. I was going to manage Donna's death the way she managed her own life.

Donna and I talked about nothing, and I'd call friends and family to come by and visit, though it was harder for Donna to get it up for company now. She would engage but withdrew easily. It's hard to be Donna when you are wearing a diaper and dying. I tried to be the host of the death talk show, welcoming guests and keeping the conversation going.

It wasn't until day seven on the unit that one of the nurses, one of the more supportive and caring nurses, told me Nina could come visit. I brought her from home and she got on the bed with Donna and fell asleep. But by this point Donna was not fully aware of the world around her. She drifted around like a small white dandelion seed floating in silence, looking to alight on a new surface and start over.

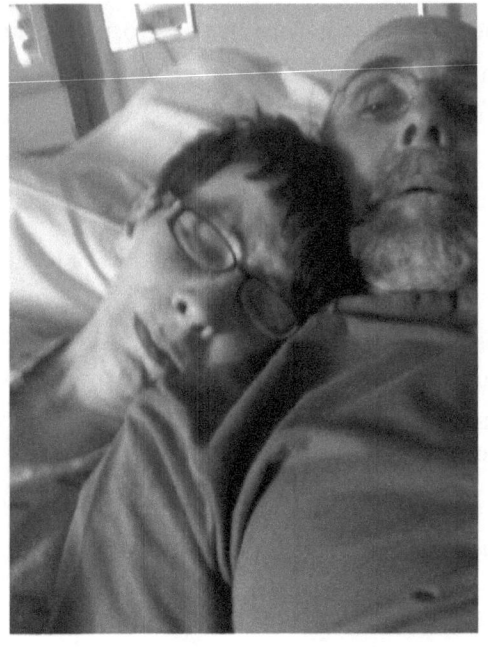

A few times I tried to sleep in Donna's room. The staff would have set up a bed. I didn't want to trouble them so I sat in the chair across from her and watched and waited to fall asleep with her and share a dream. No luck. I stayed wide awake, thinking. This was not our bed. This was not our home.

Sometimes I'd read to her or play
music on her iPhone. Her playlists and
albums were mostly Donovan, Joni
Mitchell, West Side Story, James Taylor,
Edith Piaf, the Rushmore soundtrack,
and Keith Jarrett. I hope she heard.

> Her dementia was getting worse and in the
> evenings it was acute, exacerbated by sundown
> syndrome. She became agitated, irritable, and
> demanding, losing her glasses while they were
> on top of her head, yelling at the staff if I
> wasn't there. If I were at home they'd call me
> from her phone since she couldn't work the
> screen, then she'd lace into me about how I
> ruined her phone or locked it.

As night fell she'd calm down and rest and we'd
talk a bit. This must have been the scene at
Stonehenge when the sun set, everyone looking
up and screaming for the moon to appear and
tell the earth that the day was good.

Hospice Saved My Life. The staff and all the support members knew to the nth degree why Donna was here and what I was going through. Perhaps some of that was because Donna and I knew what we needed and wanted and expected. "The kindness of strangers" rang in my ears.

Still, there were moments when I was frustrated. It wasn't till week two that I complained to the social worker that I was tired of hall meetings to discuss Donna's death. After that we spoke in her office or the chapel.

There were also some very Donna moments, even now. A group of trained Hospice volunteers would come around to ask if I needed anything, a coffee, if I wanted to talk, if Donna and I would just like them to spend time with us, being comforting. One volunteer wore a black vest littered with random pins, buttons, and symbols. He came to Donna's bedside and introduced himself, adding, "If there is anything I can do, please let me know. If you want to talk, I am here."

Donna looked at him and said quietly, with sincerity, "Go away, you are creepy looking."

I guess the vest was not as Chanel as she would have liked. I'm sorry that man got the full-on Donna but it was such a relief to see her be her.

"Now would be a good time to have end-of-life discussions with her," the Hospice Rabbi and social worker said. "What does she want for her funeral? What are her regrets? Did she find joy in her life?"

>Joy? I failed her.
>All I could do was think of that.

I hesitated for a day. Then next afternoon, alone in the room with Donna, I looked at her in the bed and said, "Donna, perhaps you want to talk about your funeral."

>She looked over at me and said, "Don't be a maudlin pussy."

>Then she rolled onto her side and fell asleep.

I made the funeral plans in two days. I was an account manager executing a tactical plan for a client, bang bang bang, do do do, keep moving so I don't drown.

August 5th, a Friday night, Donna was mostly sleeping on that razor edge of death and euthanasia. Her extensions were a mess. She looked like hell and I was ashamed I let her get to this point. I had failed yet again. I took a picture and texted it to the woman who was doing her extensions.

"Help, can you come."

There wasn't a response right away so I called her and pleaded with her to come and fix Donna's hair. Being around the dying is not something any of us want. Death seems contagious. But Pamela came to the room. She was visibly shaken, seeing Donna in this state, in a bed, not conscious. She opened her bag and pulled out scissors, a spool of microfilament, and some gel. Then she took out each extension, brushed it, replaced it, and with the skill of a surgeon, tied the extensions to what little hair existed. I'm not sure Donna felt better. I did. I guess I did.

You've got to love Facebook and their wonderfully painful service called "memories." Here's one they popped up on my feed, something I wrote that evening:

> Donna had a crisis today. Her extensions were undone and she was upset. Pamela came by tonight & made it all better. Even on heavy meds Donna smiled and said she loved Pamela. It really touched both of them to make this small yet beautiful connection. The kindness and love that has been embracing us is touching. Chart note: tell her how beautiful she looks. Not hard to do under any circumstances.

Sunday evening I was finishing up
with Nina when the phone rang.

> "Come back to the hospital right away.
> Her breathing is agonal."

Shallow breathing means death.
I jumped in a cab and told the
driver where to go and how. The
moron took a wrong turn near the
hospital. I jumped out and raced
down the pavement, through the
hospital to her bedside.

I was late. Donna was lying there with her eyes closed. The light of the evening was filling the room, empty of life. I sat in the chair next to her bed, not surprised or shocked. I kissed her. The nurse came in and said she passed away five minutes ago.

An attending and a resident came in to pronounce the time of death. They brought with them extreme understanding, kindness, and empathy. I tried to comfort them but failed, and cried for the first time since her diagnosis.

As the sun was setting, I left the hospital and sat in the park across the street, facing west. You could see the orange sky nearly to New Jersey though the valleys between buildings. I began to call family and friends, but suddenly realized that two blocks away on 18th Street, that was where we were married 28 years before. I remembered the Rabbi saying during the service, "Marriage is one life event we do together. We are born alone. We die alone."

Donna was alone while I was running to be by her side.

DEATH

I was afraid no one would come to her funeral. I was afraid that no one would remember her. I had to get on the phone, make sure people would come, arrange the location, order food.

I did not stop to consider the beauty in her death, the beauty of what was and is and the darkness of what was to follow. Today, I wish I'd taken more photos of her in that early evening room. Held her longer. Stroked her hand in death.

I was all tasks, all failure.

Donna's memorial service was Wednesday, August 10th, at the Greenwich Village Funeral Home on Bleecker Street. It wasn't until two days before the funeral that I realized it was a block away from where we'd lived together on MacDougal Street, before we were married and the first few years after. We'd come full circle.

That day, walking to her memorial service, I relived the Friday nights we ate at Monte's on MacDougal. The Saturdays we shopped for mutz at Joe's Dairy, fresh pasta at Raffetto's on Houston Street, coffee beans at the Porto Rico Importing Company, prosciutto at Faicco's Pork Store on Bleecker. The afternoons we just window-shopped in Soho, until we came home with a bag or two anyway.

I told the funeral director to expect about twenty-five people. Nearly a hundred came.

The Rabbi from Hospice presided. He had not known Donna aside from those last two weeks so I asked him if I should have friends send him thoughts on Donna to help with his service. He wrote back,

> ... good idea. My remarks will be brief for those that truly knew Donna will always be the best equipped to deliver a eulogy. Not withstanding that fact—for me it would be important to have her closest friends "paint a picture" of Donna's essence: her passions, interests, qualities; her character and relationships. What made Donna special in their eyes; her complexities; what made her tick. The idea is to describe the "whole" person in an honest, truthful and honorable fashion. I hope this helps a bit to start the process in developing a sketch of this wonderful lady—your wife Donna.

Five years later I am still sketching.

I said some clumsy words at the service.
I don't think they're worth repeating.

Her friend Joe spoke in great detail about her and their friendship. Here is a portion of what he said:

> *Donna was a complex, gifted, intelligent, and often misunderstood human being. On the outside, she was edgy, tough, and unflinchingly direct. Let's face it; sometimes Donna could be a real bitch. But she never asked more from those around her than she did of herself.*
>
> *If you were lucky enough to be let in, you could see the down-to-earth, vulnerable Donna just beneath her protective armor. She could be a demanding taskmaster; a sensitive little girl; an inspiring mentor; and a loyal, genuine, and unselfish friend. She was fierce, dignified, and unsentimental in her battle to survive cancer—right to the end. In many ways she beat the odds—living more than two years beyond her expected prognosis.*
>
> *For whatever reason, Donna saw something special in me—and in her own generous way, she made me feel better and more confident about myself. I was one of the lucky few she let in. And for that, I'll forever be grateful. I am so proud to have known her—and so proud of all she accomplished in her too-short life. I love you, Donna, and I'll miss you. The world is going to be a little less stylish, a little less organized, and a lot less honest without you.*

Everyone came to our apartment for food and drinks afterward. There were perhaps forty people; my friends tease that when I have a dinner party it is eight people max. Any more than that throws me into a panic.

This was warm and touching. It held me together. The apartment was filled with friends and family talking and smiling. There is that damn reflex of when someone smiles you smile. The kitchen island was filled with food, wine, ice, paper plates, cups, and desserts. Like our wedding it was a party, but only I was invited. Donna could only be there in our thoughts and words.

The next day I began the process of getting death certificates. On the phone, making calls, I'd glance around the apartment and see her in the artifacts, the art, the items she carefully and painstakingly selected. They were not objects but her, re-embodied.

I began to write thank-you notes to everyone and thought of Donna writing her Christmas cards.

I closed her credit cards. Or thought I did. A week later I received a letter from American Express expressing their condolences for my loss and telling me they closed her account for me. I was confused. How did they know? The cards I'd closed, I knew I didn't talk about her death. This year I learned that most credit card companies review Social Security files of recent deaths. Apparently, they match those deaths to card members and close the accounts.

My grief was a bas-relief I
ran my fingers slowly over.

Many friends and neighbors invited me to join them for dinner. It was a welcomed chance not to be home, though I felt secure at home. These meals with others were my chance to speak about Donna.

Then, two Fridays later, I walked into the local sushi restaurant where Donna and I would meet after work on Fridays. We always soaked in that moment when we began to let the week go, knowing the next two days were ours. Friday evenings were magnets on our refrigerator, holding notes that captured our lives.

The waiter who usually served us saw me and held up two fingers.

My mind screamed at him, "God damn it, don't you know Donna died and you are doing this to me now!"

Then, "Sorry, Donna passed away after being sick. Thank you for thinking of her." But that was only in my mind, too.

Finally, I just held up one finger. Since that day, when I go there they don't ask, I don't tell.

THE STALKING HORSE CALLED GRIEF

Say hello to My Little Friend.

This is the buddy road trip sequence of the story, starring MLF and me. Which is funny because the two of us used to be Donna and me. How far things have come. Or not.

MLF started to pal around with me when Donna was diagnosed. My Little Friend was passive and sleepy at first, as I filled my days with managing the disease Donna handed to me.

Perhaps MLF had been with me forever, just a nucleotide in my DNA. Prior to her diagnosis I had set a goal of not suffering if I were ever struck with a terminal or debilitating illness. I don't want to be a burden. When Donna said Oregon, I knew what she meant.

During Donna's treatment phase, Dr. B. gave me a card for CancerCare.org and the name of a contact. I went through counseling with them until 2010. She was winning the battle then, and I was doing well so I stopped my sessions.

Then she died, and MLF was present and proximal. In the pale morning light of summer, MLF was there.

In the dark of that winter, MLF was still there. I used to share the bed with Donna. Now My Little Friend sat there all night, and every morning it let me know my options.

I would see clothing or an item in a store window that would be the perfect gift for Donna for Christmas. MLF would say, "She would love that sweater. You know how much she liked sweaters. The color is perfect too." Or about a bag, "Oh, look at that. The size is so perfect, and the shape."

As I walked around the city, I wasn't imagining seeing Donna. I only wanted to do something for her, with her. It was my attempt at caregiving for someone who had died.

I'd see an elderly person at the gym working out slowly and cautiously, lacking the energy and drive of the young.

"Seriously?" MLF would wink and smile. "You want to be that?"

I would sit at my desk at my consulting gig, staring at the Hudson River, thinking about how meaningless and unfulfilling my work was.

Suddenly, startling me, MLF: "Hi!"

I wrote to my previous counselor to tell her about Donna's death and she invited me back. I went for a few months. Once I asked her about statistics of spouses dying spontaneously and naturally soon after their partners.

"That only happens with the very elderly."

As those of us residing in this world know, there has to be a plan and it must be well considered, clear, with an achievable outcome. MLF was the perfect project manager. We reviewed my life like a spreadsheet. We chatted about the columns and rows and what was going into them.

"I should clean out the house and sell everything so nobody has to do it when I'm gone. I don't want to be a burden."

"Let's make that column one," says MLF.

So I did. Who is column one and Gets What is column two.

"I should figure out how and where I use you."
"Let's add that to the list," says MLF.

So I did. I thought through all the possibilities. I even chose exactly how and where from the possibilities, and moved those tasks onto the Completed page.

"I should write good-bye notes. Which will suck because they all have to be personalized. I'm a marketer, I don't personalize."

"Okay, that'll be column three, Notes For Personalizing," says MLF.

"Do I have to write notes? It just means I'll be remembered for a low IQ, bad spelling, shitty grammar, and terrible tense usage."

"Well, it's not like it matters, Mark, because in two days you'll be 'you who?' Add it to the list."

MLF and I listened to an NPR/Fresh Air interview with Sam Parnia, M.D., about his book Erasing Death. It was a spellbinding episode. At about the thirty-minute mark, Dr. Parnia said that ninety percent of patients who have died and been resuscitated do not report any experience while dead. Ten percent of them, though, do attest to having had an experience, and most of them say there is nothing to be frightened of. Death was a positive moment for them. Wait for it: Dr. Parnia then noted that these were all patients who died of natural causes. The ones who committed suicide and were resuscitated describe an entirely different experience, a nightmare, frightening, dark, and painful.

"Holy shit. I have to do this once and do it right."

"Yup," says MLF.

"Well, I'd better skip this little romantic ideation I've got going with you and get serious!"

"Why don't you just redefine 'natural causes'?" says MLF. "She's never coming back and you can join her any time. Perfectly logical. Perfectly natural."

I had failed Donna. I watched her fade and wilt and die for three weeks in Hospice. She handed me her disease and I dropped it. Life, knowing this, was more than I could take.

My Little Friend watched me, listened to me, walked through my days with me. At a time when I couldn't make the simplest decisions, MLF gave me the power to make one choice, every day. I could be with Donna any time.

And I still can. MLF is still with me. We still discuss the spreadsheet.

"What if I'm one of those people who gets the nightmare when I die? What if they don't bring me back and I'm stuck in that horror?"

"Consider this," MLF says. "If you fail to die, whatever happens can't be any worse than your life these days."

"Some days," I say. "Not all my days."

Because MLF isn't always here anymore. Sometimes I weigh the worth of my week by remembering how many days MLF didn't appear.

MLF has asked to say something:

I agree with what Mark is describing, but will add that I am not here to drive a resolution nor am I expected to fix this. My role is simply to be a conduit to channel the reality of his life. When Mark is busy and with friends I fall by the wayside. I am not sure that is because I am no longer needed as much as, perhaps, it is a masking effort to keep others clear of me. I am not evil. I am a rational choice.

ALL THAT REMAINS

I feel powerless over my grief.

I ride past the spot we biked, where she rode alone, and I imagine her having that yogurt she sent me the picture of. I look around our home and see what Donna created for us in its design, style, and detail measured to the very inch. On Sundays I prepare dinner, glancing to my left where Donna set the table with linen napkins, serving plates that match the settings, all the silver, and I say just loud enough, "Donna!"

The hand mirror she used to check her hair sits on her vanity. I pick it up—she saw her reflection in it, why shouldn't I?

I look at her calendar to confirm dates and see there are no entries after July 10, 2011. I find Filofax calendars from the '90s with work appointments, vacations, little red hearts on my birthday.

I find receipts in saved grocery bags.
"She was alive that year."

Each individual memory is clear. All these objects, images, and thoughts feel like shards of bone in her ashes and they cut me.

I need to stop sifting her ashes in my mind and taking those cuts, but I won't consider closure. That would mean blindly ignoring all I've learned and felt. Closure would remove these memories both small and large. It will leave me stranded in a limbo between two realities. I won't waste the gift of grief-scented love.

Donna loved me into being. I liked what she saw in me. I liked being what she wanted me to be. Frequently, I was my best through her eyes. That living mirror is lost.

That is not to say I am not whole or complete. I just don't see myself. I don't recognize what I am, what I will become. At some point and in some fashion I need to let go of who I thought I was to become who I am or want to be.

I've pushed and pulled all of these memories like drops of mercury into one narrative silver drop, to see what I have not seen: if not a meaning, then at least my face, upside down, reflected in a single convex drop, looking back at me.

Who is it that I see in this quicksilver? I need to accept that I am turned around, pointing in a new direction.

The world we created was a good place to reside. I craved the grief spurred by my memories. It brought me closer to Donna and anchored me, and kept me from moving that final appointment with MLF onto the Completed page.

Or so I thought. After five years of reckless reflection on my loss, it is clear that even in death, Donna has given me so much. What she gave me while we were together and after her death exceeded the sum of my parts.

Meeting Donna was a single moment of chance in a lifetime of randomness. From that grand accident, we evolved. The best of our DNA entwined and we became something new, individually and together.

All that remains are these memories, our lives, her illness, her death, my mourning, and my grief. I no longer consider them burdens of hurt and pain. They are the gifts we gave each other. Mine is open, the wrapping paper and ribbon torn off, the gift shining within. I still carry that DNA. It is all I need to survive.

I see my memories differently now. They nourish my soul so I can move forward. I am recalibrating myself with my new DNA, never apart from Donna. What is clear is that I am committed to taking these memories with me, and creating new ones.

I quietly whisper in the quiet house:

"Donna, forgive me for exposing you to the world like this. I was afraid I was forgetting you. I needed to see you once more."

"Donna, I am sorry I couldn't save you or save Nina. I tried. I did my best."

"Donna, my broken parts that hurt you have healed. It may be too late for you to feel that."

"Donna, sometimes I wait in the dark and listen for your key to turn the lock on the front door. I know it's foolish but I wait."

"Donna, are you waiting for me?"

ACKNOWLEDGMENTS

Josephine Diamond, a neighbor, comparative literature department chairman, and dear friend. Josephine spurred me on to write this book. Her motivation brought this book to life.

Clare Gailey, the editor introduced to me by Jo Diamond. Clare was more than an editor. She elicited from my heart what was hidden. Editors edit. Clare inspired. Thank you.

Philip Johnson, book designer. Phil had a daunting task. Design a book about a designer, creative director, type maven, and my grief. He captured both my words and Donna's memory in a way that I know would make Donna proud.

Ron Furedi, a long time close and dear friend who took a final review and offered his clear, smart, and sensitive direction to make this book better.

Spotify for making it easy to create Love Letters to Donna playlist user name saltypleiades.

Thank you all.

www.ingramcontent.com/pod-product-compliance
Lightning Source LLC
Chambersburg PA
CBHW031059080526
44587CB00011B/744